ᴇXHILARATION

To Order This Book Please
Contact the Author at:
ragdoll4u@msn.com

EXHILARATION

Carol Cade

iUniverse, Inc.
Bloomington

Exhilaration

iUniverse books may be ordered through booksellers or by contacting:

iUniverse
1663 Liberty Drive
Bloomington, IN 47403
www.iuniverse.com
1-800-Authors (1-800-288-4677)

ISBN: 978-1-4620-4522-8 (sc)
ISBN: 978-1-4620-4524-2 (hc)
ISBN: 978-1-4620-4523-5 (ebk)

Printed in the United States of America

iUniverse rev. date: 08/22/2011

Endorsements

The Creator has bestowed upon Carol the most wonderous of gifts...the ability to reach out to others from the heart by sharing her own personal experiences. I feel humbled and blessed as I read the eloquent poetry of Carol's gift, as it uplifts and gives courage and hope to fellow survivors. I will look forward to meeting you and showing you our beautiful traditional territory.

Cathryn Paul
Tia'Amin First Nation of the Coast Salish People

Carol has an unique way of writing that provides a refreshing honesty about life. Her candor, insights and wisdom engage the reader in a delightful and emotional experience. This is Carol's second book and just as much a treasure as her first. Thank you Carol for sharing your gift and your life experiences so eloquently.

Bett McLean, BA
Trauma Therapist
Couples Counsellor
Life Coach

I am not a reader of poems. I have never really understood poems and therefore have avoided them. When Carol's first book came out and she asked me to read it, I thought I would do it out of obligation and that would be the end of it. When I got home with Moments of Reflection in hand, I sat down to read the first one. Then the second one, then just one more and before I knew it, I simply could not put it down until I finished the whole book. It gave me goosebumps. Some made me want to cry, some made me laugh and all of them gave me an insight that I never thought I could get from reading a book of poems. And now this second book is out and it just confirms what I already knew about Carol Cade. She is a very deep and spiritual person who looks far beyond everyday thinking and yet verbalizes what we already thought we knew. A must-read for every person who reads books.

Sylvia Steffens
Realtor

"Carol has an interesting way of painting real life situations with words. Drawing on her personal experiences she invites the reader to join her in exploring her inner world."

Joy Borthwick
Author

CONTENTS

The Rose.. 1

The Language of Love 3

The Man That Loves Me................................ 6

Life 8

Momma and Poppa.................................... 11

The Beginning 13

Birthday Thoughts 16

Turning Sixty-Five...................................... 18

Words 20

Hearing.. 21

The Light... 23

Goals... 25

Happiness 27

First Born.. 29

My Son 31

Banyen 33

Red Hat 36

The Gypsy 38

My Future.. 40

The Bald Eagle.. 42

Our Battle.. 44

The Chief 46

Decisions 48

Rain 50

Gus The Goose 52

Whatever Would I Do? 55

Silence... 56

Is This Progress? 57

The Chase 59

Boots 62

Fear 64

Parting 65

The Stones 67

Fender Bender 69

Sadness 71

The Soul 73

The Caterpillar 74

The Man On The Roof 76

My Thoughts 79

Time 81

The Creator 83

Why I Wrote This Second Book

It came as a delightful surprise to me that my first book—Moments of Reflection—was received very well.

I then began getting requests for a second book and gave it serious thought. I decided to "go ahead" and hope that it will give as much satisfaction to my readers as my first book has.

It had been a real "learning" process for me in writing my first book and so it is not such an overwhelming feat this time round.

I wish to, once again, acknowledge my son, Mark . . . as without him there never would have been a first book!

To be able to write down one's experiences in life and hopefully pass on some words of wisdom, as an author, is truly a wonderful opportunity for me.

Within the pages of the book you are now holding is my hope that you will return to it more than once, as you find various poems that may be up-lifting to you or, just a source of pure enjoyment.

Remember, it is never too late to go after your dreams and make them come true!

Thank you to all that requested this book.

May all that read this book be blessed.

Dedication

I wish to dedicate this book in memory of my foster parents who
provided me
With the foundation for my life—

Violet and Philip Walthers

Special thanks to

Mike who always works so hard to keep my special food
well stocked in order to give me "energy" so I might direct it to my
writing.

Thanks to Laverne Utterstrom who stood by my side as I again
put pen to
paper—your support has always been endless.

Thanks Also To

All of my faithful pals that took the "time" to read through my
poems once
again and gave me their feed-back . . . so much appreciated!

Acknowledgements

There are some very special people I would like to take time to mention now. These people have all affected my life in many ways.

Mark Hulstein—My son, who will always remain close to my heart.

Bett McLean—Who has helped me more than any other person I have met.

There never has been a truer "friend" than Bett. I can rely on her 100%.

Linda Furness—Who is always "here" for me when I need her. A true comfort she has been in my life.

Denise Bevan—Whose battle with cancer helped me change the direction of my own life for the better.

Wendy Johnston—A delight to know as we have spent over 40 years together

And she is is always ready and willing to help me out.

Valerie Sallenbach—My dear beloved friend since we were 5 years of age.

She always is here to give encouragement and support.

Maleen Lavachek—Who I met on the computer some years back. A true and Loyal friend indeed.

Carolyn Bradley—A real lady that knows how to truly "listen." Thank you!

To all of the above people I just say "thank you" because each and every one of you have added richness to my life.

The Rose

I saw a purple rose
It stood so tall and true
I wondered where it would lead me.

Isn't that a funny thought to have about a rose?
Still the thoughts remain stuck in my brain.

This rose was a gift
Given to me on a "special day."
As I sit here and write
It's fragrance gives me delight.

A "purple" rose is like no other
And I was gently "reminded" that that rose represented "me."
It is an overwhelming thought indeed!

A red rose represents "love"
But, what does one say about a purple one?
It's beauty outshines the others
Because it stands out you see.

I wondered then if I stand out like that?
Do others see me standing tall and straight
Even though I am only five feet!

This rose gives me "hope"
As I still must stay afloat
And rise above life's iniquities.

So when I feel down
I shall remember this rose.
It stands so gracefully.

The petals open to receive abundance from all good things as it
reaches for the sun.
So must I stand with arms held open and wide
As I look to a higher place
To raise me to a place of grace.

This rose withstands the strife that abounds.
It is a good reminder to me to stand my ground.

And, so for the one who gave me this rose
I say "Thank you" from deep within.

THE LANGUAGE OF LOVE

Look around you
See the sky so blue
The grass so green
How about the color of the leaves on the trees?
"Nature's Wonderland" is a paradise indeed!

You feel the gentle touch
Of your spouse's hand as he caresses your face.
After a hard day of work
You both rest in an embrace.

You start your day with many "small" deeds
As you sow love as you plant your seeds.
You dust and clean
Cook and scrub
So all is nice for the one you love.

He returns to you from a hard day of work
Toiling to earn the money to keep the roof over both your heads.
He washes the dishes after the meal
Once he has settled, with newspaper in hand
You place his feet on the footstool to rest
And bring him his coffee as a treat.

This is a man that is strong in his love and not weak
He shows it in many ways.
His shoulders are wide and there for you when you need to cry.
He gladly shares any burdens that are on your mind
His ability to "listen" comes from his heart.

When you are ill
You know he is there to help you through the pain
He will cheer you on when things go right
And be there to pick you up and dust you off
As your world comes tumbling down and crashes at your feet.

The examples above I have written down
Are all "samples" of the "language of love."
And here are more thoughts for you to ponder as you read.

A "smile" does wonders
So you make it a practise
To give that smile to brighten people's day
As you hurry along
Spreading more love in a different kind of way.

To the elderly people you meet in your day
You give them full respect
And listen to what they may say.
For once upon a time
They also were "young" as you are now.

They have "experience" from life
And you may learn something nice
If you will only take the time to hear what they say.

The "language of love" can be shown in many ways
Designed not only for our family and our mate
But to others who we may only glance at once and never see again.
Give out what you can in kindness and love.

The beauty of Nature
Is also God's "language of love"
As He gave us so much for us to enjoy.
Let us savor it and take joy in what we see each day.

Never to forget that the "language of love"
Goes on for a very long time.
Let us make sure we show some each day as we go along our way.

The Man That Loves Me

I have a man that loves me
He remains a mystery in many ways
As I do not see what he find of interest in me.

He is intelligent and while "on the surface" he remains "cool"
On the inside is quite a different kettle of fish
As sometimes inner turmoil resides within.

His "elusiveness" was of great interest
When first we did meet.
And yes, I found it a challenge
To see if I could break through that invisible wall.

He is known for his stubbornness
But that is now in remission
As I fought it with much aggression!

To make a relationship "work" it takes two
Thus we have learned to be partners in all we do.
This man that loves me has plenty of charm
He can chat the ladies up as I stand and watch.

But, it is just his nature to have fun.
I can trust him, so do not run.
His love is one hundred per cent sincere and his devotion true.

"Mystery" can attract
For one never knows what lies under it.
Certainly it is a trait that can pull like a magnet.

This man I love has a great sense of humor
His laughter comes from deep within
His eyes do twinkle
As his smile expands.

He has no enemies
As he is a friend to all.
Smart with his hands
He can fix or make just about anything.
He is very artistic in many things.

So I sit by his side
And listen while he talks
We end our days quietly
As we each share our thoughts.

The heat is turned down
And the lights go off
As we snuggle together to get closer.

It is with much satisfaction
As I lie within his embrace
I welcome the sandman as slumber overtakes.

ꟿLIFE

What do you know of "strength, courage, integrity and life?"
Can you stand on your feet when you are weak from sorrow,
sadness and pain?
Do you dare get up again as your heart still bleeds from the arrows
of meanness
Others did bestow?
What of the illness you suffer from—has it taken all your strength
and made you
weak?

It is your choice to lay down quite still
Or fight the dark shadows that threaten to take you down
Can you claim your "strength" again?

How well do you stand in the face of adversity?
Are you able and willing to hold your ground
When those around you try to bring you down?

"Courage" wears many faces.
Our strength of character shall show on our faces
When attacked from all forces.

When you voice your opinion to those things you know are wrong
Be well prepared to exercise self-control over the ignorance of
others who set out
to do harm.
"Courage" can be found in the "silence of the tongue"
And not in taking forceful actions, as if out-of-control.

True courage comes from deep within
To withstand the evil that tries to slip in.
You must stay "alert" while you go through these tests
Knowing your "courage" brings true victory in the end.

Now what of "integrity" do you know?
Are the words you speak and the actions you show
Indicative of a person of true integrity?

If put on a stand in front of a judge
Would "integrity" shine from deep within,
As the words you utter, are they an example of what I speak?
Or, would you "compromise" integrity just to keep the peace
And therefore escape the judgment of man at the words you just spoke
Knowing someone will suffer from the honesty you spoke.

If "true integrity" is a part of you
All those who know you
Understand you are one that keeps their word
And never betrays a confidence given.

They say "life" is never easy.
I am here to say it depends on how we choose to view it.
Life throws all kinds of things we would rather not endure.
Your true character can be enriched by these trials.
Even though you wish you could escape it.

What is "it" that matters most to you in life?
Is it wealth, possessions, travel and adventure?
Or, is it things unseen—such as "deep peace" that lies within.
The "joy" you experience when you see that first smile from the
baby you bore.
What about your eyes that can see, the nose that can smell and the
ears that hear?

Take time to think on the words I wrote
Strength, courage, integrity and life.
Strive for the absolute "best"
Because then your soul will truly be at rest.

Momma and Poppa

For my momma and poppa
Whose home was never a mess
I truly was blessed
They picked me to add to their nest.

I was only three months of age
When momma took me to her house.
You see, I was a foster child
And her gift was to take those that needed a place.

I recall the many that came and wept when they left
As they were to go on to another place.
For they left behind a home full of grace
That is something hard to replace.

Momma's dream had always been to run an orphanage.
Her heart was made of gold.
The love she gave was something one could never replace.

Luckily my poppa shared her point of view
Because he never knew how many children he would come home
to at the end of the day.
A gentle, quiet man was he
Who would take me on his knee
While yet another story he would read to me.

I learned how to say my prayers
As I would watch my momma kneel each night
Too give thanks for her blessings that came from above.

How many countless hours did she hold me and rock me the
whole while
As yet, another illness I survived.

I have written this poem to pay my respects
To both my momma and poppa
Who long ago did leave this Earth
But will always live forever with each breathe I take.

I was wise enough
While both were well and alive
To make sure I told them their worth
And to tell them how grateful I was for all their work.

Truly I had been blessed
To have been given such a strong foundation
Built on love and devotion to the family they had chosen.

Wherever they may be
I say still, "Thank you for all you gave to me."

THE BEGINNING

Did you hear the baby crying at the top of her lungs
As she laid in the dresser drawer where she had been placed?

Did you see the next door neighbors racing to the phone
To call the "authorities" to check on the noise next door?

The Children's Aid Society came in haste
The tiny bruised baby was now safe.
They took her away from the abuser that had hurt her
She was the "girlfriend" of the mother that did not want her.

She arrived—at what would be—her "permanent" foster parents
place.
So tiny and frail
They thought she might fail
And not make it as the night drew near.

They had not counted on this baby's strong will
As they struggled to help her keep her nourished and fed.

They looked on with horror
At her wee back
It had been burned from cigarettes
As she had been used to butt out the burning ashes.

These foster parents were full of love and kindness
For this little baby placed in their nest
They doubled their efforts to make sure she got lots of rest.

Gradually, in time, this baby did flourish
Her start in her world had not been easy
But prepared her for all the many trials
That would lie ahead.

As a young girl
Her hair now thick, black and long
It hung to her waist
Two pig tails tied with bows at the ends.

You may wonder, "Whatever became of this child?"
Let me tell you as I write
The infant in this poem is "me."

I have survived many dark corners in my life
Meanness from others, rejection, cruelness and hate
All cast upon me seemed my fate.
I stood tall with each blow
More determined than ever these disasters
Would never stop my goals.

Life does not always give us an easy start
At times it is just a chore
As we meet—head on—with yet another disaster
Which is meant to trip us as we go.

I still struggle at times to ease the pain
From the tall shadows of my past
As I travel my path that is now full of light

I try not to look back and think on my past
But "live in the moment" and move forward with grace.
To those of my readers whose lives may be hard
Take it a day at a time and try to move on.

My "achievements" in my life have been many
Despite the obstacles I did face.
Do not give up on "hope"
If you look hard enough you will find a rope
It will help you along as you grope.

Birthday Thoughts

T'was the eve of my birthday
And I wondered where to go
As it was night
And I was all alone.

The thoughts of past birthdays whirled through my head.
Some memories were good, but others I did dread.

As one gets older you do tend to ponder
And as another year looms ahead
I am left to think about what path shall I wander.

Tomorrow holds a "new day" and the start of a "new year" for me.
I shall mark this occasion with true friends, indeed.

The years that have gone have left their mark.
I did grow in wisdom, but it was not a lark.
I now can put to good "use" the knowledge I learned
To guide others to hopefully not err, as I had in my youth.

Birthdays use to be "fun" I seem to recall
When in my youth life seemed to be a ball.
Upon growing older I found I would rather forget I was another
year older.
How I wish I had been wiser.

Never look back too much in your past.
It is better we live in the "present"
Or we risk losing what is most important
And that is the "time" we have to still do some good.

So, on my birthday tomorrow
I shall face another year full of "unknowns"
But, I shall have no fear
And it will be with joy that I blow out the candles.

Celebrate your birthdays
No matter what your age
Rejoice that you lived another year
And look only "forward" to the year that lies ahead.

Turning Sixty-Five

I went along my merry way
This lovely day in May
For you see my sixty-fifth birthday awaits me.

I wonder what lies ahead
As I wandered on my way.
The path I trod had lovely border of flowers.
They could not help but make me smile.
Perhaps I would walk another mile!

Turning sixty-five is a big thing for me.
How often can one look forward to being a "senior citizen?" says I.

The time has come for me.
And so the future I face with glee.
I thought how we cannot turn back the hands of time
So we have no choice but to move forward and face the Golden
Years with grace.

As I continued my walk—alone in my thoughts
I glanced above to see the sky so blue
And I felt the warmth of the sun on my face
I saw a squirrel run up a tree
And heard the birds sing happily.

I decided when I turn sixty-five that I want it to be a "memorable
year."
One I can look back on as the first year as a "senior citizen."
Hoping the memories I make will bring a smile to my face.

My eyes are still clear
The teeth are my own
The ears can still "hear"
And my walk is steady.

I plan on still making my life count and contribute in any way I
can to help mankind.

I find it a challenge as I look at sixty-five.
It may be only a "number" as some do say
But to me, it is the start of another part of my history.

Help me celebrate as I face this time with joy.
Let us spread happiness and still say, "Oh boy!"

Words

I love to sit and write
The words that just seem to come into my head.

I often wonder where this comes from.
However, as long as the words are given
I allow my pen to travel on the paper
Hoping whatever I deliver here
Might be advice others seek after.

Do you ever sit and wonder how a poet's words are given?
Are poets "creative" or is it combined with talent?

Whatever the reason
I am glad I have come into my season
Where writing has become my own creation.

Finally I have found my "niche."
Where before I relied on my crutch
As I was tangled in life's problems
My life was passing by in a rush.

I sought to clear my path of unwanted debris
So I could spend more time on just "me"
And now you see a "poet" in me
I am happy as can be
Long last my goal has been seen!

HEARING

I have poems that come from my heart.
Where the words come from is like a chart.
I follow the chart and see if my words rhyme.
It is like a compass that sometimes points me to the sky.

I plunder through the darkness in my head
Hoping to find the correct words that are wise and will blend.

The darkness clears and the light now appears
As my words are given "color" my pen quickly travels
So I do not lose sight of the words in my head.

"Poetry is not easy," some have said.
I nod my head in agreement as I shake my head
Marvelling over the fact that somehow the word "poet" has been
stamped on my head.

To "what" or "whom" can I give credit for this gift?
I search deep within and can only come up with one thought in
my head.
My ancestors have been exceedingly kind to me
I truly believe the words that you see
Come directly from them as a "link" I have become.
As they dictate their words to me is a gift I use cautiously.

For the poetry I write
Is for all mankind
To bring everything that helps living be full, free and full of grace.
Life is not meant to be weighed down with heavy burdens and
grief.

The Great White Spirit looks down from above
Using as many as he can to do the job well.
I have been blessed as "one" of the chosen.
And thus try my best not to fail this test
As my pen travels over this paper so fast
As the words now given must not be lost.

In reading my poems
May peace reside.
Know that one "strong in spirit"
Is always by your side.
Open our arms wide
And let him enfold you if you are wise.

The Light

I knelt on the floor
As I said my prayers
Deep in thought and heavy was my heart.

I prayed for all those who were fighting for their lives
And thought of their families who waited their fate.

My tears flowed as my prayers just did not seem adequate
When suddenly a light did appear
And I found myself bathed in it's glow.

I did not move and kept my head still bowed
My hands still clasped as I prayed.

I heard a voice whisper gently in my ear,
"Do not feel your prayers are going unheard.
For the Father above hears "all" that is prayed with love.
Your prayers and those of many others, rise to His throne as
incense.

Be assured if all who prayed
Did do so with true love and sincerity
The world would be a better place."

I felt the warmth of this wonderful light
And absorbed all the love that emanated from it.
It seemed to fill each of my pores
And I suddenly felt stronger than ever before.

I stayed on my knees for quite awhile
Kneeling in silence, as the light had become my companion.
I was hoping it would not leave, as I hungered after it
As my soul had been thirsty and I did not know it.

As the night wore on I sensed it was time for this light to now
leave
But I heard the voice for the last time saying to me,
"Be strong and of good courage. Pass on to others this knowledge
you have learned from me.
All prayers are sufficient to do wondrous things.
The Father hears and accepts the pleas of those whose hearts are
pure with
Love for others."

And with these words the light did fade.
I felt uplifted and not afraid.

So, I pass these words to all who will listen.
Never cease praying for yourself or others.
The world is in deep chaos
But with your added prayers it can decrease.

Let us lift each other up in prayers
As they ascend on the wings of a dove
To the Father's chair.

GOALS

I sit at this table all alone
Lost in my thoughts that swirl in my mind.
The day seemed so short
Time had just fled.

The plans I had made
Had faded away—as the rain came
And spoiled the day.

My life seems to be passing
Like a car that is racing
I still have much I want.
Places to go—travel is in my mind.
But, will I ever have the time?

I reflect on my life that thus far has passed
And am left wondering how much of it do I have left
Before I can accomplish my dreams at last.

I feel very much "alone" as I write on this page
As we each are in charge of the direction we take.

I stand at the bottom of a very steep hill
To climb it will drain my energy within
As I already battle the fatigue that sets in.

I realize that we are all really "on our own"
As we journey along the path of Life.
And to reach our goals, all else must be pushed aside.
Glance neither to the right, nor to the left
Keep your eyes fixed "straight ahead.

When "weariness" sets in
Rest if you must, but do not give up the dreams you carry deep
within.

If you "give up"—you loose
However, if you can lift your eyes beyond what pulls you down
You will find the mind will clear
And once more your goals are still there.

Feeling alone as you battle this fight
Tests your strength as you press on.
You will learn to use the time wisely
As you conquer the problems that seem to be in the way.

Try to remember how wonderful you will feel
When the goals you set before you
Are no longer dreams
But have now become reality!

HAPPINESS

There is happiness
That lies deep within
It flows like a river
That has no end.

I revel in this fact
And wonder, "Is it just an act?"

As I searched my heart and looked in my soul
I found real peace was abound.

A genuine smile broke out on my face
It felt like a true miracle had taken place.

You see, it had not always been this way
For the path I have travelled
Brought me much grief
A smile was never on my face.

"Time" brought many changes.
With the trials I grew
As I turned my face to a higher place
My faith started to grow.

The dark shadows of sadness
Soon got lost in the light
As I heard the word "serenity" whispered in my ear.

The "Father" above looked down on me
Soon He was sending many blessings my way.

Overwhelmed with gratitude
I knew my soul had stretched in latitude.

My "frowns" had really been
Smiles upside down!

I hang on to my happiness
With both hands held tight
As I fling my worries in the air
And watch them disappear.

"Happiness" rules
"Sadness" is gone.
Three cheers for me!
I am happy indeed.

Do not let "life" get you down
Remember your frowns are really
"Smiles" upside down!

FIRST BORN

Moments of time go fleeting on by.
I remember gazing into your eyes
Your black hair was long and silky to the touch
The tiny fingers curled into a wee fist.

My "first born" were you.
A marvelous sight!
I had to blink twice to make sure you were all right.

Wrapped in a pink blanket
You felt so soft.
Content to lie sleeping
As the world revolved.

There is nothing that can compare
To a mother's first sight
At the lovely child she beholds in her sight.

With skin like velvet
And that "fresh" new born scent
Your eyes shut tight against the bright light.

My tummy felt hollow
Where once you had been
Was now strangely empty
And all was "quiet" within.

No more wee toes stuck in my ribs
All movements had ceased.
It was a strange feeling for me
As "birth" brought you into the world
But left me empty within.

I bent down to bury my face in your wee neck
With gentleness did I kiss the top of your head.

I knew your father was as proud as could be
For at long last his wish for a daughter had now been complete.
And thus I bowed my head and gave "thanks."
For there is no greater miracle than that of giving birth.

Some moments in life we do forget
But never the first time we give birth.

My Son

I thought to myself, "What a wonderful experience to hold a son."
as I gazed upon your face.
The nurse had just bought you to me
And laid you gently on my breast
Feeding time had arrived and you were all set.

I already had a daughter
And now had been blessed with my son.

As I looked at your tiny face
I smiled as I saw the beginning of a curl
Right in the middle of your forhead.

Your arrival into this world
Came three weeks ahead
As you were anxious to start your life
Forget about "schedules"—you ran your own race.

You were a happy baby
Full of laughter and smiles
Your response to the outside world
Was always fast and quick.

As long as your tummy was full
And your diapers clean
You never fussed nor were a bother to me.
A happier baby I had never seen.

Your childhood past swiftly
Soon your future was ahead
"Decisions" had now to be made
As you prepared yourself for schooling ahead.

With much thought
You decided your course.
So, with a full nine years of college
I held my head proudly and watched you graduate
With a law degree now stamped after your name.

From the wee baby I first held
You have now grown to a man
Who holds his own power in his hands.

Education and intelligence were your "spice of life"
You ran the full circle with the choice you made.
You were wise in your decision
The choice you made was filled with wisdom.

BANYEN

I had a cat named Banyen
She ran among the trees
Her feet were swift as rabbit's
Her eyes as sharp as could be.

She had a magic about her
You would have loved her—as did I.
She was low to the ground as her legs were so short
And her tummy jiggled from side to side
As she frolicked along the way.

She was such a precious cat to me.
Her love of flowers bought her much delight
As I often found her lying among the petunias
And she had flattened them out like an ice rink you would see to
skate on.

She was part "Manx" you see
So "short of tail" was she.
Her yellow eyes so large and soft
Her gaze would make your heart stop.

She never did hiss, scratch, fight or bite
It was not part of her nature you see.
She had a gentle soul
And wanted to live a life of peace.

In the years I was ill
She was always near
To offer me her comfort and body heat
As she would know exactly where I hurt
And gently lie upon that painful spot.
It gave relief to me.

For fifteen long years
This role she did play
My only companion
She helped me in those days.

When her time came to depart
It was with great sorrow in my heart
To say, "Farewell to one I loved."
My grief was heavy and my heart felt cracked.

But, Banyen was a very magical cat
And not one to see me suffer with loss
To my delight and surprise
The very next day
A "visit" from her made my day.

I had just had my lunch
And arose to put the dishes away
Much to my surprise my eyes spied
A pile of dry cat food
Two separate colors did I see.

Upon further investigation I opened my close closet
Where the shoes were kept
Only to find the food was also in them.
What a mess!

I went about and cleaned it all up.
My mind wondering, "What was this all about?"
The following day, at exactly the same time
There sat the dry cat food on the same spot.

I picked up a few pieces and put them on my kitchen counter
It helped my mind to know this was a serious matter!

The following day I waited in anticipation
But, alas no food again ever showed up.
What I have written here are "true facts."
My beloved Banyen showing me she really had not gone.

For those of you who grieve for your pet
Remember my words and try not to forget
Our furry companions may lay at rest
But be assured they do live on
And still watch over you yet.

Red Hat

I have a red hat—many in fact.
I wear them everywhere
Except to bed.

You see, I belong to The Red Hat Club.
This club is for a group of ladies that want to have fun.

We adorn ourselves in red and purple.
I grab my red boa and fling it over my shoulder
My feet quickly slip into the red shoes that await
I hastily leave and head out the gate.

My friends are waiting.
What a colorful sight are we.
Many heads turn as we walk down the street
For how often does one see so many dressed as we?

Our luncheon is ready.
It is with much laughter and smiles as we take our seats.
The food is delicious
The ambiance superb!
Our chatter goes around our table
Like a top that never stops.

And then the real fun begins!
The cameras are taken out
We must capture these happy moments.
Some of us poise in funny positions
While others are too busy getting their nutrition
Forget about "smiling," the food is delicious.

It is great fun being a Red Hatter
As friendships are made
And we all know we will be there for one another
In cases of serious matters.

So if you are feeling down
And want to get "out and about"
Join the Red Hatters
You will soon see what laughter is all about.

THE GYPSY

I am a gypsy that has travelled far and wide
My life has been full of adventures of all kind.
From my caravan windows much I have seen.

Eagles flying high above, circling in the sky
Wild life surrounded me as I went along my way.
Often I felt the grass beneath my bare feet
As I wandered the fields in front of me.

I have always wanted to see the world
To stay in "one place" was not my style.
In my blood is the need to run
And "freedom" is the name of my game.

As a gypsy I moved from camp to camp
Sitting by the light of the fire at night
I would re-count the day and all I had seen.

I have been in places where the sun was hot
I would gaily run on a beach
As I headed to the water as the sand left my footprints behind me.

With much joy I would dive in and feel the coolness of the water
come over me.
I would splash about and kick my feet
And the child within came out to play.

I would lie on my back in the ocean deep
And look up at the beautiful blue sky
Where there was not a cloud in sight.
What a relaxing way to spend my day.

When the Seasons changed
And the rains came
I remained safe and dry within the caravan.

The rain would turn to snow
But I never felt the cold
I always had enough heat
There never was coldness in my feet.

I do not travel alone in this caravan
"Gypsies" are we all
Who share our life in peace
As we travel along our way.

I would not change my life for anything
There is much still I wish to see
The gypsy in me shall see it is done
Would you like to travel with me?

MY FUTURE

What lies ahead I do not know
For my future flows like a river
Full of bends and twists
Where it ends remains unknown.

There are many questions left unanswered
And as I search for the truth
"Disguises" shall be revealed
And all "masks" dropped.

The "secrets" that are still hidden
Will be opened to the truth that awaits.
For those that kept me for so many years in the dark
Shall find themselves in the bright light as justice will prevail.

When all is unveiled and the truth shines forth
Then my true future will unfold.

I will grab the truth and all it holds
And run with the wind
As nothing now can stop me.

I shall fly in the air
Like a bird with wings
I will sing a song of freedom
With arms lifted up in thanksgiving
My voice ringing loud and clear.

The angels on high
Shall hear my song.
Their wings gently flapping
As they look down from upon.

With a face now radiant
And eyes so clear
A heart now full
And a soul at rest.

I have fought my battles
For my future to be sublime
I celebrate the obstacles that stood at my gate
Because I managed to destroy the enemies that had threatened my fate.

Whatever your battles in life may be
Stand up for your "rights"
Because there is always someone higher that will bring your enemies defeat.

You cannot "win" if you choose to stay hidden
Get out in the open and fight for your rights
You will grow strong and your knowledge will take flight.

I wish you the best as you journey through life
You will gain your self-respect if you stand and fight!

THE BALD EAGLE

I flew as high as my wings would soar
And found myself perched on top of a tall tree.

I looked down to see the view.
The water was calm
Not a ripple could I see.
The sun shone brightly on me.

I glanced down to the right and saw many people relaxing
On blankets or chairs—as the case would be.
This is a place where many came to rest.

The world looks different from here on high.
Not nearly so crowded with people rushing by.

I much prefer being in the sky.
Did I mention the fact I am a bald eagle?
Some say I am "majestic" others say I am "strong."
Others stare in awe at the span of my wings as I glide along.

I am noted for many things.
In some places I am revered.
In 1782 I became the emblem of the United States of America.
How is that for popularity?

My eyes are sharp
My jaws like a wrench.
I swoop down quickly on my prey.
They do not stand a chance.

To live a life as a bald eagle
You must be strong
For we also have our enemies
That would like to see us gone.

OUR BATTLE

I sat astride my horse
The wind was blowing my hair off my face
As we galloped along the way.

In the saddle I sat up straight while
I tightly held the reigns.
My horse's hoofs thundered along
As we tried to keep up with the rest of the throng.

Our trip was a mystery
As we did not know where we belonged.
Thus we rode our horses
In hopefully a better direction
So we could set up camp
And settle and take a well deserved nap.

We no longer lived in a peaceful land
It had become an area from which we ran.
We had taken our women and hid them away.
"But, now what would become of us?" we say.

For the white man has arrived on what was "our land."
And we now found ourselves being driven away.
It had become harder and harder to find safety.
We needed a plan.

Finally we found a place of shelter.
We set up camp and gathered around
We had built a fire to keep us warm
As we sat brother by brother, arm in arm.

Prayers were offered to the Great White Spirit
As we joined our hearts and souls in this serious matter.
"Grant us direction and your protection," we prayed.
"For tomorrow is yet another dangerous day."

Early in the morning we arose
The fire's embers now had grown cold.
We dismantled the camp and armed with our bows, arrows and spears
Once more we took to our horses and mounted the saddles.

Whatever we had to face
We knew it would take courage
As our days were now full of peril.
Still we were determined to try and keep our land.
With this goal in mind and our will to survive
We rode in large numbers, side by side.

We had been here a long time
Before the white man had arrived.
We knew we would lose many in battle
However, a strong nation we had been
And knew in time we would be strong again.

Eventually the white man would respect our ways
As we would become as educated as they.
Doctors, lawyers and teachers too
We would manage to keep our culture true!

THE CHIEF

The eagles rise and the spirit soars
As I raise my face to a place unknown.
My long black hair lies wet on my back
As I have just emerged from a lake in which I swam.

I come to this spot often
For silence and meditation.

Sitting on the ground
With my legs crossed
I sit with my hands in my lap.

When I raised my head and my eyes looked up
It made me feel good to see the eagles above.

I come here often for guidance from above.
You see, I am a "Chief" of a Native Band
My responsibilities to others is widespread.
Therefore I must not err in the judgments I must hand down.

In the land where I dwell
There is much unrest
It must not erupt and cause more mess.

I consider "all sides"—as I listen to The Elders
And the council of the wise.
But, in the end it is "my words" that give the final advice.

Today as I came to my favorite place
I sought help and a "sign" that my pleas are being heard.
Then I saw the eagles flying so high
Their wings spread wide as they circled the sky.

I felt great humbleness as I observed all this
For I knew then the Great White Spirit was by my side.
My responsibility as being a "Chief"
I knew would be guided by the one on high.

I rose to my feet after awhile
Feeling stronger inside to face my people and our trials.
I gave "thanks" to my ancestors who watch over me
I was ready now to face my day.

DECISIONS

I sit here in my chair
Searching within my soul
Wondering, "Which way should I go?"

Decisions are not easy
For they can change the course of your life.
Do you want to sink or swim?
Then one must take care to see how deep the water is before you
step in!

Is your path smooth and easy
Or is it full of pot holes
That make you queasy?
You must pick up your feet
So you will not slip and slide into defeat.

I ponder why in life there are times we are faced with difficult
decisions.
Sometimes, because of anger, I turn crimson
As I wrestle with my decisions.

What has life taught me thus far?
Can you provide me with a compass
So I can see which way to go?
You see, I do not want to get lost and bogged down in mire.

If my pockets were lined with gold
I would be more bold
And head off to adventures unknown.

Alas, such is not the case.
So, I will pack up my troubles in my old suitcase
And hit the road and see what I will face!

RAIN

The rain is coming
And it drowns my sorrows
I now can look forward to a new tomorrow.

I thought there was no gold at the end of the rainbow
But have found I am wrong.

The rain is coming!

The rainbow's end is such a lovely sight
It makes me glad as I sit and write.

To find true happiness
Is such a delight.
Look around you and take in the sights.

"Real" happiness resides inside.
Now look deep within
Surely you can find something you can revel in.
There should be a smile now as you think.

After the rain stops
The air is fresh
The grass is wet.
Do you feel refreshed?

Is your heart full
And the soul "nourished?"
Is there "hope" for you
As you face tomorrow?

The rain does always come
Just as the sun
Look at the day
And go have fun!

GUS THE GOOSE

I am a white goose
Who is on the loose.
I wander through the bulrushes
As fast as can be.

For you see—something is chasing me.
Alone am I in this situation
Wondering if I will survive.

"Ah." Says I. "The water I see."
If I can only make it then safe will I be."
I was on my way to fetch my mate
When all of a sudden I had to run
The predator was trying to catch me.

I decided to take a chance
And ran as fast as can be
Because then I knew "air borne" would I be!

Before I knew it I had lifted off the ground.
My wings held me up
And I flew with delight
Because the predator was below
And I had my height up in the sky.

I should explain I and my mate
We are kept as special pets
And me in my silliness
Went out the gate!

They call me "Gus" and my mate's name is 'Hanna."
The people we dwell with are so kind
They have children that feed us all the time.

Hanna caught my eye one day
As I was flying in the sky.
I glanced to my right
As I "sensed" someone else also had taken flight.

Lo and behold—there was lovely Hanna.
T'was love at first glance we did share.
From that day on we were a pair
We had never left each other's side.

Until today when I got myself in a pickle.
I glanced down below to try to find
The dwelling place where Hanna and I reside.

At last, at last! I saw the red roof of the top of the house
Where the people were inside.

I flew in that direction
And landed safe and sound on solid ground.
Hanna was running around squawking my name out loud.

"Gussie, Gussie," she said. "Where are you?"

"Here I am." Said I.
She hurried towards me
A big scowl on her face
As my disappearance had caused her to race all over the place.

I managed to smooth her ruffled feathers.
She had decided I was, after all, worth all the trouble.

The children when they saw me
Rushed with a big bucket of food.
I ate until I was full.

Hanna and I then sat side by side.
Peace had been restored.
I had been such a fool
I have learned my lesson to never venture outside the gate!

WHATEVER WOULD I DO?

Whatever would I do if you should die?
Never to see your deep brown eyes
Or hear the laughter that comes from deep within
To see the smile that makes me "grin."

Whatever Would I Do?

"Life" has been kind to us thus far
That we would meet in such a way.
Let us not take for granted these sweet hours
For we do not know the exact hour this will end.

Whatever Would I Do?

Whose arms would hold me and give me strength
Or offer comfort when I can no longer fight?
Your feet are planted on solid ground
You are a man I can count on.

Whatever Would I Do?

I cannot count the many ways I love you.
The feelings run deep and the words won't flow
To fully express all that I know.

Whatever Would I Do?

So while we still have each other
Let each moment count
To relish every day we have been given
Knowing our love only grows stronger as we get older.
Let us sit and watch the lovely sun set.

SILENCE

"Silence is golden," isn't that the rule?
I have found it to be so true
For in the quietness you can hear your heart beat
As you rest and perhaps contemplate.

To find a place of silence
Is something I relish
For there I can refill my empty batteries
So once "full" I am then ready to face anything.

I love silence—as I take in nature's gentle sounds.
The birds chirping in the trees
The rustle of the leaves as the wind blows ever so gently.
The sounds of traffic now far away
Something I do not miss in my day.

Too much noise that surrounds me daily
Tends to make me rattle and the nerves do shatter.
And all that matters becomes cluttered in my head as I seek my
place of silence again.

The wounds that tend to bleed within from the world's problems
And the soul that seems empty
All can be resolved in my place of silence.

I welcome the gentle breeze on my face
Alone in my chosen solitude
As I lay on my back and rest at last
I lie on my blanket that covers the soft grass.
Silence is so refreshing
Won't you come along and share this blessing?

Is This Progress?

I was lying relaxing under a tree
And glanced around me to see what I could see.

I saw a lovely hanging basket
The flowers so graciously draped over the side
Their fragrance did fill the air
Their scent was heaven sent.

I turned my head to the right
And my eyes landed on a different sight
"Towers"—many of them, stood so tall
I remembered when that land had bushes and trees.

I wondered if this is what is called "progress"
As we strip our land and knock down trees.
We drive out the animals that gave them shelter
The starving coyotes are seen by many
As well as bears now come into the city.

What has "man" done to the land we live on?
What of the many animals who have lost their homes
Where do they now go?
What food is there left for them to eat?

I preferred to think of the hanging basket
And the beauty of the flowers
Rather than dwell on all those towers!

I am left to wonder
If man and all his power
Is destroying our Earth with all the towers.

For the bit of nature that is still left
Take it not for granted
For we know not how much time we have
To fully enjoy what the Creator has blessed us with.

These thoughts ran through my head
And I made myself promise to delight
In what was within my sight
Before it is all stripped away.

THE CHASE

I dropped my hat
And I never looked back
A strong wind whipped like a lash that snaps.

I felt the rocks beneath my feet
As I hurried down the street
To escape the one who was rushing to try to catch me
As if I was a thief.

I drew my cloak tighter as I fled
And everything at my feet did scatter.
Darkness was starting to come
My eyes strained to see what was ahead.

My breathing was labored
And the legs were feeling heavy
As I raced down the cobbley street
My mind was scattered.

It was Winter and I was cold.
The mist had started to roll.
Still I knew I must move
As being pursued was no laughing matter.

I sensed the stranger behind me coming nearer.
I choose to race around the corner.
In fact, you see, I am a good person indeed.
Why I am being chased is beyond belief.
Tis nothing I did wrong to make this dreadful thing happen.

As I rounded the corner
I thought I might flounder
As my foot caught on something
And to the ground I did clatter.

I strained to get myself off the ground
As the chase was still on.

Panting now, my feet on solid ground
I continued my hasty pace.
I could see my house not far away.
If I could just reach it
Inside I would find safety.

The stranger was nearer now
I felt him grab the cloak that I wore.
I released my tight hold
And could hear it tear as it slid off my back.
Still I did not look back.

I was getting weary
And so glad to see my home now near.
My pursuer had fallen back—my cape in his hands.
I took this as a sign to keep up my fast pace.

Finally I reached my front door.
I quickly found the key and entered my place.
The sweat was dripping off my face.
I had actually won this chase.

I peeked out my window
And no one was in sight.
I exhaled a huge sigh of relief!

It became quite clear to me
One should not wander down unfamiliar streets.
As you may also find yourself in a race and being chased!

BOOTS

Boots and I live in a shack
Down by the railroad tracks.

He is a big cat
With large yellow eyes
His coat is always shiny
But he is far from tiny.

Boots is black in color.
His four paws are white
And he has a very long tail.

Of all the cats I have had
He, by far, is my favorite.

I am a hobo
So we do not live a life of ease.
I wear a "coat of many colors"
Just like the song you may have heard.

In the evenings when it is dark
We sit by the fire I make to keep us warm.

Boots is happy with anything you feed him.
Lucky for me, since our food can be scarce.
And when it is time for sleep
He snuggles beside me as we fall asleep.
Many a night I drift off listening to the purring beside my ear.

The life of a hobo has "no schedule."
So we arise at our own leisure.
I spend my days looking for bargains
For people do throw away the strangest of things!

Although I may not be rich in some people's eyes
I feel I am, as I still have my health
I get lots of fresh air and exercise
As I search around for any kind of rewards.

One day I found a can of cat food.
I hurried on home to present Boots with this gift.
Upon opening the can and placing it before him
His eyes lit up and a big, loud "meow" came out of his mouth.
This was his feast for the day.

I would not change my life
For this is all I know that is.
Boots is my best friend
He relies on me and I on him.

Our life is simple
We like it that way.
It does give us time to play.
Life without Boots would never be the same.
A hobo I will remain.

ᚠEAR

I lie on my bed and lie in "fear"
As the thoughts whirl in my head.

"Tread lightly over me," I silently pray.
As I feel my feet are made of clay.

"A cat scan?" you say.
"Oh yes." Said I.

"I worry what the results may be."
For it is always the unkown that makes our heart miss a beat.
Still I must be able to stand on my feet
And not give in to defeat.

Fear is a terrible thing
As it tries to fill our mind and soul
I grasp every single, positive thought
To try to keep me steady as a rock.

The fact remains I must just "sit and wait"
Until the results I see.
The fear hangs on like a cloud over me.
I fight to see the sunshine as the darkness covers me.

The days seem long and the nights are worse
As it is in the "silence" that the fear does lurk.
Grant me strength to get through this time
So I can conquer "fear" and stop the tears.

Parting

I hug my pillow as close as can be
As I look over at the spot where you use to be.

I gaze through my window and see the stars
Wondering where you are.
Can you see what I see?

For so many years you were by my side
To "part" was something that never entered our thoughts.
But, as life would have it
"Death" played his part.
As he took you away and it broke my heart.

I lie and weep in sadness
The dark shadows do surround
As I think of your casket in the cold ground.

Where does one go to escape this sadness?
This sorrow and grief is torture, not gladness.

The memories of the love we shared
And the life we had together
Only makes your absence that much more bitter.
Just like a cold winter that makes you shiver.

Is there "anyone" in heaven above
That can help me in my despair?
What of the loneliness I now feel
How do I cope with the emptiness of my bed?

Suddenly I am aware of a "presence" nearby
That puts a "stop" to my rattling thoughts.
I heard your voice, ever so gentle, saying in my ear
"Did I not tell you I would never leave you?
I am here and will wait for you till it is your time to journey to the
other side."

Hearing your voice and the words now spoken
Made my senses aware there was nothing to fear.
As our love had held us together
I realized it now still held true.
Because Death had taken your body
But your soul was still active and alive.

I drew comfort from these thoughts
And had finally found some release from my grief
I knew then I could finally sleep
And the dreams would be sweet.

THE STONES

I put my hand in my pocket to see if they were lined with gold
Only to discover there were nothing there but stones.
These were "special stones"—with unique power.

I carry one that was to draw abundance and wealth
The other was to keep me safe.
So far they have worked for me.

It was quite by accident you see
That I ran across the magic of stones.

Peering into a jewelry case one day
My eyes laid sight on a lovely Sugalite.
It is a purple stone and it beckoned to me.

I took it in my hands quite reverently
For it's beauty was something rare indeed.
Deep down in my heart I just knew I had to have this Sugalite.

With great delight I brought it home
Only to discover it had "hidden" wonders beyond belief.
It is a stone used for healing and spirituality.
As that is what I expected I put it around my neck.

As I gazed at this stone
To my amazement I could see other figures of people showing.

"Could this be really true?" thought I.
"Maybe my eyes are playing tricks on me."

I got out my trusty camera and took some photos.
Thinking all the while, "These people won't be seen in these
photographs—you will see.'

However, that definitely was not the case
Because they showed as clear as crystal
Causing me to know this Sugalite was special indeed.
I felt very "blessed" to know that whenever I wear this lovely stone
The people within are there to be my guardians.

So, if you ever come across some stones
Treat them with awe and respect
For one never knows what to expect!

FENDER BENDER

I was rounding the corner
Unaware I was about to get a major fender bender.

It came from out of the blue
As in haste I did hit the brakes.
I felt my neck jerk and thought
"Oh my, my. Here we go again."

This was the second time my neck
Had been put into serious pain
I was not looking forward to what I knew lied ahead
To get relief from this pain.

So I managed to get out of my car
As did the other person who had damaged my fender.
The usual procedures were done, as phone numbers etc. were
exchanged.

With reluctance I got back in the vehicle.
Managed to start her and headed in the direction I wanted to go.

Once at my place
I took a look at my fender
And with an expression of disgust
Decided from now on maybe I should take the bus!

An accident can happen quite suddenly and be cruel
As I am sure many of you know.
But you still choose to drive too fast
Taking great risks to many around you.

Take heed to my words
You do not want an accident to majorally change you in ways you
would never suspect.

Be smart and use your head.
Putting your foot hard on the pedal
May seem like harmless fun.

But, in the end everyone suffers
And some lives could end.
Do you really want that responsibility on your head?
Slow down and live!

SADNESS

There is a deep well of sadness within me
From where it comes I do not know.

The soul is lonely and I feel like not facing tomorrow.

Do you ever feel this lonely?
Or are you one of the lucky ones
Who only reads about it in poems?

The man I love is not here.
There is no one to give me some cheer.
So I sit here all alone
Wondering how much further must I go before I can feel whole?

What does my tomorrow bring?
Dare I even open my eyes as the dawn breaks?
Suppose there is no sun to see, but only the darkness as the sky is
full of rain.
Will this lift my soul?
I highly doubt it.

I look forward to my dreamless sleep
As the night creeps on and soon I will go to my bed in hope of
finding peace.

I draw the covers close to my head
As I relish in the warmth of the bed.
"Alone" I may be
But I can escape under the blankets that gently encase me.

The man who supposedly loves me dearly
Has taken this night to be wholly on his own.
His sweet loving words are soon forgotten
As I lie in this bed and am left to wonder
"Is this where my sadness started
When he decided not to be by my side while I fall into slumber?"

I say to myself, "What does it matter?"
So what if my heart feels shattered.
I can choose to stay with my sadness
Or get on with my life and all that really matters.

"Be strong," I say.
This too shall fade away
Tomorrow is another new day.

I reluctantly will lay down my pen
As I realize it is now time for bed.
I will quiet my mind while I nurse my heart.
I have made up my mind that tomorrow is mine
And will allow no sadness to enter my mind.

The Soul

The "soul" is an interesting topic—don't you think?
It resides in each of us
How it evolves is a mystery.

When each of us depart
From this place called "Earth"
The body returns to dust
But, the soul lives on for eternity.

What do you think of your own soul that dwells within?
Or, have you even stopped to think about it?
Are you too full of hollow ambition
That it keeps you from looking at your soul's condition?

It is a major part of "who" we are
And have no doubt
For the day will come when each of us must give account
For the condition of our soul.

I write these words for all concerned
To give "encouragement" and take note
To try to shine up your soul
Just as you would polish your shoes.

Leave no dust or dirt in the soul
So you may stand on judgment day
As your soul shines as bright as the sun.
And your face reflects gladness because you won!

THE CATERPILLAR

I approached the base of the tree
And looked way up high and thought to myself,
"Oh my. It is so high! Can I do the climb?"

I felt the roughness of the bark
As my feet started up that tree.
I took it slow—as many feet have I.

I noticed the branches as they spread their limbs far and wide
All covered in beautiful green leaves.
It was that time of year when all things were in bloom.

You might wonder why I would choose to do this climb
When it was easier to stay on the ground.
But, I was safer up high from my enemies that roamed below.

Many know I feel warm and fuzzy
I am never known to hurt another.
Many a child has picked me up
To watch my gentle way as I walked on their arm.

We are harmless creatures
Our wish is to never hurt another.
In "peace" we wish to travel on our way
Especially as I climb this tree.
It was a very warm day as I journeyed up that tree
Since it was not my nature to hurry
I enjoyed all I could see along the way.

The color of the leaves—oh—so green.
The sky so blue
Shadows from the sunlight filtered through.
The ground below was covered in dust.
How much cleaner the air was above!

Finally I reached the top.
I breathed a sigh of relief
It was time to curl up on a leaf
And catch up on my sleep.

So, the next time you do see a caterpillar
Think of me and the tree.
Remember to be kind to us.

Please do not stomp on us and crush us on the ground.
Rather choose to step aside and let us be on our way.

For you see—as time goes by
As a caterpillar something "beautiful" does arrive
Where once a lonely caterpillar was I
In the end I shall turn into a beautiful butterfly!

The Man On The Roof

I saw a man
Sitting on a roof
Leaning against a chimney stack.

He had a pipe in his mouth
And out of it came billows of white smoke.
On his head he wore a cap.
I wondered what he was doing up there.

He saw me peering up at him
And lifted his arm and waved cheerfully
A smile was upon his face.

"Who are you?" I yelled from below.
"I am here on a mission," was his reply.
A mission from a rooftop!—What a strange place indeed!

The man continued to smoke his pipe
As his glance took in all he could see.
He seemed to be so much at peace up there
I hesitated in further interruption of his "mission."

"You see," he said, "I can see so much more from up here
Than if I was down on the ground.

I can survey the people's home and all that goes on in those homes.
For it is "behind closed doors" one truly sees what people are made of."

I marveled at what this man had said and cocked my head to hear
more.
"It is my job to see how mankind treats others and just how much
love and
Kindness does reside.
There is no better spot to do this than from a rooftop.

I have not been sitting here for too long, but enough time has fled
So I can truly say in many homes
True love, kindness, mercy and forgiveness
Are greatly lacking.
It will make my boss unhappy."

I stood below and hung my head
As I heard these words just said.
In my heart a prayer ascended
As I asked that many hearts would surrender the selfishness that
lies within
For truly it would be a high cost to pay
If all hang on to these terrible ways.

When I opened my eyes after this prayer
I looked back up on the roof top
Much to my dismay
The man had disappeared.

I thought perhaps I had imagined all this
But something caught my eye
And lying on the ground next to my foot
Was the pipe the man had smoked.

I knew this had not been just an "apparition."
A "word to the wise is sufficient."
His message echoed in my mind
Let us all pay attention.

Bring more love, kindness, mercy and forgiveness into our lives
So our world can continue and not be destroyed.

I decided to also "make this now my own personal mission."
I will incorporate those words and do my part.
"What say you. Will you do your part?"

My Thoughts

I sit here alone with my poem and wait
Wondering what more shall come through my gate?
I have fought many of life's battles
One by one, and for the most part
Won them with my heart not completely shattered.

My life is not easy and never has been
For it seems to be my story
"Alone" and searching for glory.

Sometimes I search deep within my heart
Looking for the answers to fill the empty spot.
Still my hands are empty as I reach for the stars
My gaze is focused on heavenly places
I only need to lift the veil and see all the places.

The Lord above knows my heart.
He had His eyes upon me right from the start.
His arms held me up when I wanted to fall
His words of wisdom would echo within when I thought each
problem too tall.

Without His love I would have been defeated
Instead I came out stronger as I fought and crawled through my
darkest hours.

Now I sit with my chin in my hand
Alone with these thoughts that tumble through my head
Remembering so well many tears that flowed
Brought on by circumstances beyond my control.

I tried so hard to duck my head as the arrows of cruelty were
coming my way.
"Be merciful dear God." I did plead, as I felt each piercing of the
arrow that hit my heart.
My soul did bleed with each cruel blow
While I wept in solitude alone in my bed.

In the darkness of the night
I held on to the blankets tight
While I swallowed the pill of injustice
And wondered how to fight.

I learned without the trials in my life
The person I now am would not exist.
I did overcome the meanness of others.

It was not an easy task
As I choose to not take revenge
Nor hold a bitter thought.

I truly believe that those that threw those darts
Will one day find they will sink in the mud
With many of their own problems not forseen.

With this thought in mind
I found I could last.
If you can remember "we all have a choice" in how we decide to
react
You also can come out victorious.

TIME

"Time" is a precious gift
Do not let others steal it
For once it has gone, you cannot retrieve it.

We all need our "own space" to do our things
Whether it be just to sit down on a swing
As we move our legs to and fro
Feeling the air as it blows through our hair.

There are those who would choose to use us
They prey upon us like vultures
Running away with all we have
To eat our food, ask our advice or steal our money
And in the end we find we have nothing left to offer
Our "time" got used up and another day wasted.

To learn to say "no" is a craft we must master
If we ever hope to have the "time" we are after.
We can only give so much to others
Then set the boundaries and become our own teacher.

It is not a selfish goal we are after
Wanting some "time" for laughter
That we choose not to share with others
But to nourish our own souls in the silence as we sit under a tree.
Alone with our thoughts can bring nourishment to the mind
And rest to the body, that perhaps has grown old.

So take my words seriously
Make the "time" for yourself
Because if you do not
Others will have taken it away.

Your arms will hang by your side
And your gaze will be down.
Your mind full of other's troubles
Your face wears a frown.

The body now needs rejuvenation
As the mind is now cluttered
It also needs a rest—as it is all muddled.

So find a peaceful spot
Lay your blanket down
Let your thoughts wander and ponder
This is now "your time" to rest!

The Creator

I looked down from my place above
There is much I saw that brought me dismay.
So much damage man has made.
It made me sad to think this way.

However, I did see many on their knees
Praying for others and many things.
Seeing this fact gave me thought all is not lost.

My Son sits to the right of me
As we watch to see how mankind conduct his ways.

There is always celebration when a new baby is born.
Or we see a mother teaching her young how to bow their heads
and they pray.
Their tiny hands clasped together
So innocent in their ways.

It is with heavy hearts when we see "man" enter the church—our
house of worship.
Only to be there to fill a seat
When in their hearts there is no authenticity.

Still there are many others who never come to worship
But know the truth of what is preached
And live accordingly.
These are the ones who do not live with hypocrisy
And thus their prayers are crystal clear
Sent straight from their hearts.
Their answers are soon received.

My Son paid the highest price ever asked to save all mankind.
He did this in obedience and set the example we must "trust and obey"
For the Father knows the way.

His death was not in vain
As all know He rose on the third day.

I hope the words that are written here
Do pierce the hardness of the hearts of men
And open the eyes to see and the ears to hear.
Let your soul awaken
And rejoice in all that awaits.

To those that live in "darkness" what can I say?
For my Son has shown you the way.

Man's days are "numbered" and life is short.
I have given you all "freedom of choice."
It is not my way to force myself into your life.
I will wait patiently for your "invite" to dwell within and let you live in "light."

.